POEMS THAT
LIVE AND REMEMBER

Poems are a way of saving the best parts of the things that happen to us, because they capture forever the feelings that go with the memories—

> *how wonderful it is to discover*
> *you're in love,*
> > *how awful it is not to be able to*
> > *say it,*
> > > *how good and terrible first*
> > > *things are . . .*

We reach out to one another, and the words are ready to be said—

> *are you afraid?*
> > *do you remember?*
> > > *does it have to be this way?*

But time's against us, and so we sometimes only speak to each other much later, in poems.
For this collection, Richard Peck has brought together over seventy poems—each the sharing of a very private moment, each the beginning of a very special memory. . . .

Pictures That Storm Inside My Head

poems for the inner you

Edited by
Richard Peck

AVON
PUBLISHERS OF BARD, CAMELOT, DISCUS, EQUINOX AND FLARE BOOKS

PICTURES THAT STORM INSIDE MY HEAD is an original publication of Avon Books. This work has never before appeared in book form.

AVON BOOKS
A division of
The Hearst Corporation
959 Eighth Avenue
New York, New York 10019

ISBN: 0-380-00735-5

First Avon Printing, October, 1976

AVON TRADEMARK REG. U.S. PAT. OFF. AND IN
OTHER COUNTRIES, MARCA REGISTRADA,
HECHO EN U.S.A.

Printed in the U.S.A.

✒ Acknowledgments

JOHN CIARDI "Sometimes Running," "Counting On Flowers." From IN FACT by John Ciardi. Copyright © 1962, Rutgers, the State University. Reprinted by permission of the author.

THE CROSSING PRESS "You Understand the Requirements" from BLACK APPLES by Lyn Lifshin. Copyright © 1971 by Lyn Lifshin. Reprinted by permission of The Crossing Press, Trumansburg, N.Y. and the author.

DOUBLEDAY & COMPANY, INC. "Frankenstein by Mary W. Shelley" from SHRINKLITS by Maurice Sagoff. Copyright © 1970 by Maurice Sagoff. Reprinted by permission of Doubleday & Company. Inc.
"Child on Top of A Green House," copyright 1946 by Editorial Publications, Inc. from COLLECTED POEMS OF THEODORE ROETHKE. Reprinted by permission of Doubleday & Company, Inc.

DAVID ETTER "From A Nineteenth Century Kansas Painter's Notebook" by David Etter. Reprinted from GO READ THE RIVER by David Etter, published by University of Nebraska Press. By permission of the author. Copyright © 1966 by David Etter.

EDWARD FIELD "The Bride of Frankenstein" from VARIETY PHOTOPLAYS by Edward Field. Copyright © 1967 by Grove Press. Reprinted by permission of the author.

HARCOURT BRACE JOVANOVICH, INC. "Cousin Nancy" by T. S. Eliot. From COLLECTED POEMS 1909-1962 by T. S. Eliot; copyright, 1936, by Harcourt Brace Jovanovich, Inc.; copyright © 1963, 1964, by T. S. Eliot. Reprinted by permission of the publisher and Faber and Faber Ltd.
"Ithaca" by C. P. Cavafy. Copyright, 1949 by Rae Dalven. Reprinted from THE COMPLETE POEMS OF CAVAFY translated by Rae Dalven, by permission of Harcourt Brace Jovanovich, Inc.
"The Pardon" by Richard Wilbur. FROM CEREMONY AND OTHER POEMS, copyright, 1948, 1949, 1950 by

Richard Wilbur. Reprinted by permission of Harcourt Brace Jovanovich, Inc.

"o by the by" by E. E. Cummings. Copyright, 1944, by E. E. Cummings. Copyright, 1972, by Nancy Andrews. Reprinted from COMPLETE POEMS 1913-1962 by E. E. Cummings by permission of Harcourt Brace Jovanovich, Inc.

"who are you, little i" by E. E. Cummings. © 1963 by Marion Morehouse Cummings. Reprinted from COMPLETE POEMS 1913-1962 by E. E. Cummings by permission of Harcourt Brace Jovanovich, Inc.

"Science Fiction" by Kingsley Amis. From A LOOK AROUND THE ESTATE, © 1967 by Kingsley Amis. Reprinted by permission of Harcourt Brace Jovanovich, Inc. and A. D. Peters and Co.

"So Long Folks, I'm Off to the War" by Anthony Ostraff. Copyright, 1954, by Anthony Ostroff. Reprinted from his volume, IMPERATIVES, by permission of Harcourt Brace Jovanovich, Inc.

HARPER & ROW, PUBLISHERS, INC. "A Character" from AFTER EXPERIENCE by W. D. Snodgrass. Copyright © 1958 by W. D. Snodgrass. Reprinted by permission of Harper & Row, Publishers, Inc.

"Morning Song" from ARIEL by Sylvia Plath. Copyright © 1961 and 1965 by Ted Hughes. Originally published in the United Kingdom by Faber and Faber. Reprinted by permission of Harper & Row, Publishers, Inc. and Olwyn Hughes, literary agent.

"On My Child's Death" by Joseph Von Eichendorff. Translated by W. D. Snodgrass. Copyright © 1960 by W. D. Snodgrass. From AFTER EXPERIENCE by W. D. Snodgrass. Reprinted by permission of Harper & Row, Inc.

"Passing Remark" from THE RESCUED YEAR by William Stafford. Copyright © 1961 by William E. Stafford. Reprinted by permission of Harper & Row, Inc.

"Theology" from WODWO by Ted Hughes. Copyright © 1961 by Ted Hughes. By permission of Faber & Faber Ltd., and Harper & Row, Publishers, Inc.

SEAMUS HEANEY "Frogman" by Seamus Heaney. Previously unpublished. Reprinted by permission of the author. Copyright © 1975 by Seamus Heaney.

DAVID HIGHAM ASSOCIATES, LTD. "The Clown" by Elizabeth Jennings. From SONG FOR A BIRTH OR A DEATH © 1961, published by Andre Deutsch, by permission of David Higham Associates.

HILL AND WANG *"Old Age Blues."* Reprinted with the permission of Hill and Wang, a division of Farrar, Straus & Giroux, Inc. from THAT SHINING PLACE by Mark Van Doren, copyright © 1969 by Mark Van Doren.

HOLT, RINEHART AND WINSTON, INC. "Birches" from THE POETRY OF ROBERT FROST edited by Edward Connery Lathem. Copyright 1916, © 1969 by Holt, Rinehart and Winston, Inc. Copyright 1944 by Robert Frost. Reprinted by permission of Holt, Rinehart and Winston, Inc.

HOUGHTON MIFFLIN COMPANY "First Song" from WHAT A KINGDOM IT WAS by Galway Kinnell. Copyright © 1960 by Galway Kinnell. Reprinted by permission of the publisher, Houghton, Mifflin Company.
"On the Wagon" from SHORT HISTORY OF THE FUR TRADE by Adrien Stoutenberg. Copyright © 1968 by Adrien Stoutenberg. Originally published in *The New Yorker,* 1968. Reprinted by permission of the publisher, Houghton Mifflin Company.
"Oysters" from THE BOOK OF FOLLY by Anne Sexton. Copyright © 1972 by Anne Sexton. Reprinted by permission of Houghton Mifflin Company.

INDIANA UNIVERSITY PRESS "Palm Leaves of Childhood" by G. Adali-Mortti from POEMS FROM BLACK AFRICA, Langston Hughes, editor. Copyright © 1963 by Langston Hughes. Reprinted by permission of Indiana University Press, Bloomington.
"The Umpire" from THE RECKLESS SPENDERS by Walker Gibson. Copyright © 1954 by Walker Gibson. Reprinted by permission of Indiana University Press, Bloomington.

LITTLE, BROWN AND COMPANY "The Sportsman" from THE OLD BATTEAU AND OTHER POEMS by David McCord. Copyright ©1953 by David McCord. By permission of Little, Brown and Company.
"Three Floors" from THE TESTING TREE: Poems by

neice 1966. Reprinted by permission of Oxford University Press, Inc. and Faber and Faber, Ltd.

"The Wise-Child" from CONFESSIONS AND HISTORIES by Edward Lucie-Smith. © Oxford University Press 1964. Reprinted by permission of the publisher.

RICHARD PECK "Nancy" by Richard Peck, from Martin Levin's "Phoenix Nest" *Saturday Review,* June 1969. Copyright 1969 by Richard Peck. Reprinted by permission of the author.

THERON RAINES "Cherrylog Road" by James Dickey. From *The New Yorker Magazine,* October 12, 1963. Reprinted by permission of the author and his agent, Theron Raines. Copyright © 1963 *The New Yorker Magazine,* Inc.

RANDOM HOUSE, INC. "Babe Ruth," "Together" from EMBRACE by Paul Engle. Reprinted by permission of Random House, Inc. Copyright © 1969 by Paul Engle.

"Drug Store" from SELECTED POEMS by Karl Shapiro. Reprinted by permission of Random House, Inc. Copyright 1941 and renewed 1969 by Karl Shapiro.

"An Elementary School Classroom in a Slum" from SELECTED POEMS by Stephen Spender. Copyright 1942 and renewed 1970 by Stephen Spender. Reprinted by permission of Harold Matson Company, Inc. and Random House, Inc.

"Julia's Room" from COLLECTED POEMS by Robert Hillyer. Copyright © 1961 by Robert Hillyer. Reprinted by permission of Alfred A. Knopf, Inc.

"The Snake" from SELECTED POEMS: NEW AND OLD, 1923-1966 by Robert Penn Warren. Copyright © 1957 by Robert Penn Warren. Reprinted by permission of Random House, Inc.

REED, ISHMAEL "Beware: Do not read this Poem" by Ishmael Reed from *Scholastic Voice,* Sept. 14, 1970. Copyright by Ishmael Reed. Reprinted by permission of the author.

NORMAN ROSTEN "Song for the Make-Up Man" from THE PLANE AND THE SHADOW by Norman Rosten. Copyright © 1953 by Norman Rosten. By permission of the author.

P. H. RUMSEY "Dream of a Black Mother" by Kalungano, translated by Philippa Rumsey, from AFRICAN WRITING TO-DAY, edited by Ezekiel Mphahlele, published by Penguin Books Ltd. Copyright © Ezekiel Mphahlele 1967.

SATURDAY REVIEW/WORLD "The Bigot" by Harold Witt. Reprinted from *Saturday Review* February 19, 1972. Copyright © March 1, 1972 by *Saturday Review*. Reprinted by permission of *Saturday Review*.
"The Survivor" by David Wagoner. Reprinted from *Saturday Review* August 7, 1971. Copyright © September 1, 1971 by *Saturday Review*. Reprinted by permission of *Saturday Review*.

DENNIS SCHMITZ "Before the Coming of Winter" from WE WEEP FOR OUR STRANGENESS by Dennis Schmitz. Copyright © 1969 by Dennis Schmitz. Reprinted by permission of the author.

SHEED & WARD, INC. "Boxer" by Joseph P. Clancy from BEGINNINGS: Prose and Verse by Various Catholic Writers. Copyright © 1956 Sheed and Ward Inc., New York.

ROBERT SIEGEL " 'B' Movie," "Miss Foster," "The Way I hear It" from THE BEASTS AND THE ELDERS by Robert Siegel. Copyright © 1973 by Trustees of Dartmouth College. Reprinted by permission of the author and The University Press of New England.

WILLIAM STAFFORD "After School: Room Three" by William Stafford. Originally published in *The New York Times*. Copyright by William Stafford. Reprinted by permission of the author.
"One Day in August" by William Stafford. Originally published in POETRY. Copyright © 1965 by William Stafford. Reprinted by permission of the author.

UNIVERSITY OF MASSACHUSETTS PRESS "Sniper" by Robert Francis. Reprinted by permission of Robert Francis and The University of Massachusetts Press from COME OUT INTO THE SUN: NEW AND SELECTED POEMS by Robert Francis, © Copyright 1965.

For Arli Epton
whose help gave
this collection
form and substance

Contents

V   touch me if you can

VI   it is sometimes summer

VII   under your permanent skin

Thinking young is a poetic device. Not kicky, faddish young that can render one season's psychedelic poster art into an instant relic. Something, some things more lasting than that. Always reserving a side of yourself for the fresh impression. Always being able to moan a little with necessary pain—even when the pain isn't yours. Always able to remember, even when you've got degrees and old war wounds and mortgages, how grim it was to be imprisoned in childhood, how wonderful it was to know you were in love, how awful it was not to be able to say it, how good and terrible first things were.

This is a collection of young poems—about being young as fact or as feeling or as recollection. Not all of them were written by poets in their youth. Some are by those looking at the young and wishing they were or glad they aren't or bleeding a little vicariously the way you might if you had a daughter and heard her up in her room late one night typing out a story: something private and precious to her. Something that involved her and her world—and not you and yours.

Another poetic device is language. Words that communicate—prose, poetry, songs, screams—the wireless impulses we keep sending out in hope of contact and response. Stephen Spender said it in THE MAKING OF A POEM:

The world which we create—the world of slums and telegrams and newspapers—is a kind of language of our inner wishes and thoughts. Although this is so, it is obviously a language

which has got outside our control. It is a confused language, and irresponsible senile gibberish.

This thought greatly distressed me, and I started
thinking that if the phenomena created by human-
ity are really like words in a language, which kind
of language do we really aspire to? All this se-
quence of thought flashed into my mind with the
answer which came before the question: A language of flesh and roses.

The poems on these next pages are written in a
language of flesh and roses. They are pictures that
have stormed inside the poets' heads—summer storms,
some of them—and tempests and typhoons too. But
they are all winds that prevail.

Part One: PICTURES THAT STORM INSIDE
MY HEAD describes some of those vivid images of an
external world. Very little ego-involved inner-looking
here: the poets look out and project their vision . . .
of black snakes, tornadoes, jays and jewelry . . . the
worlds around all of us.

Part Two: A TEN-CLAWED MONSTER expands
these visions a little surrealistically . . . flipping through
a pop culture where fairy tales go grotesque and Frankenstein's monster gets out of hand again. Of movies
and newsreels and other distortions.

The next four parts lie at the heart of the matter—
youth. You can sort to suit yourself, but the divisions
fall this way in my mind:

Part Three: IN TWOS AND THREES THEY
WHISPER PAST MY HOUSE views youth from the
perspective of their elders. It begins with a black
mother welcoming her new son into an old world.
It ends with the death of a child.

Part Four: THE HOUSES THAT OUR FATHERS
BUILT recalls the environments of childhood—the
settings for the first scenes of our lives . . . the "Sunday

prisons" of the very young and the fantasies we built to replace them.

Part Five: TOUCH ME IF YOU CAN is an album of young faces: a boy confronting a cop with fake ease. The awkward grace of girls. The first of love, the last of innocence.

Then it's gone—the young years—leaving a lifetime for reflecting.

Part Six: IT IS SOMETIMES SUMMER reflects: has anybody seen little you-i in a world that will never be what it was?

Part Seven UNDER YOUR PERMANENT SKIN plays roles. Only a few of the guises we try on in youth before a mask finally grows into place on the face . . . "The make-up man is full of faces" says one of the poems—faces clownish, dreamy, militant, bizarre. The roles we try on and the others chosen for us.

Part Eight WHY DON'T YOU WRITE? reports rapport and the difficulties we encounter in trying to encounter each other. We reach out to one another, and the words are ready to be said: "Remember?" "I love you," "Hey let's go to the movies." But time's against us, and sometimes we only speak much later . . . in poems.

Part Nine TO BE ALIVE is about life and death. Hunters and hunted. Snipers in trees and soldiers on foot. And an anonymous child's voice from a concentration camp: very young, very old.

There is one last poem, standing by itself and looking ahead. I hope it speaks to you as it speaks to me.

Richard Peck

I

---

pictures that storm inside
my head

In the beginning was the

Kickoff.
The ball flew
spiralling true
into the end zone
where it was snagged,
neatly hugged
by a swivel-hipped back
who ran up the field
and was smeared.

The game has begun.
The game has been won.
The game goes on.
Long live the game.
Gather and lock
tackle and block
move, move,
around the arena
and always the beautiful
trajectories.

LILLIAN MORRISON

From a Nineteenth-Century Kansas Painter's Notebook

I always paint pictures
of violent weather
(mostly tornadoes
with thick dragon tails
that strike like snakes),
then give them away
to queasy aunts
and quaking uncles.
Though I find peace
in strawberry sunsets,
and those May wine days
when a clover breeze
ding-dongs the tulips,
I am obsessed
with steep funnel-shaped clouds
and frightened children
who cry and run scared
through towering cornfields.
I paint only
the dark-stained pictures
that storm inside my head

DAVE ETTER

✍ The Snake

Daylong, light, gold leans on the land.
You stoke the tractor. You *gee* and *haw*.
You fed the thresher's gap-toothed maw.
Then on a load-top, high, you stand
And see your shadow, black as law.

Stretch far now on the golden stubble.
By now breath's short. Sweat stings the eyes.
Blue denim is sweat-black at the thighs.
If you make a joke, you waste your trouble.
In that silence the shout rings with surprise.

When you wreck a shock, the spot below
Is damp and green with a vernal gloom.
Field mouse or rabbit flees its doom,
And you scarcely notice how they go.
But a black snake rears big in his ruined room

Defiant, tall in that blast of day,
Now eye for eye, he swaps his stare.
His outrage glitters on the air.
Men shout, ring around. He can't get away.
Yes, they are men, and a stone is there.

Against the wounded evening matched,
Snagged high on a pitchfork tine, he will make
Slow arabesques till the bullbats wake.
An old man, standing stooped, detached,
Spits once, says, "Hell, just another snake."

ROBERT PENN WARREN

In a London crescent curving vast
A cat sat—
Between two rows of molar houses
With birdsky in each grinning gap.

Cat small—coal and snow
Road wide—a zone of tar set hard and fast
With four-wheeled speedboats cutting
A dash
   for it from
       time to time.

King Cat walked warily midstream
As if silence were no warning on this silent road
Where even a man would certainly have crossed
With hands in pockets and been whistling.

The cat heard it, but royalty and indolence
Weighed its paws to hobnailed boots
Held it from the dragons-teeth of safety first and last,
Until some Daimler hurrying from work
Caused cat to stop and wonder where it came from—
Instead of zig-zag scattering to hide itself.

Maybe a deaf malevolence descended
And cat thought car would pass in front—
So spun and walked all fur and confidence
into the dreadful tyre-treads . . . .
A wheel caught hold of it and

FEARSOME THUDS
Sounded from the night-time of black axles in
UNEQUAL FIGHT
That stopped the heart to hear it.

But cat shot out with limbs still solid,
Bolted—spitting fire and gravel
At unjust God who built such massive
Catproof motorcars in his graven image,
It's mind made up to lose and therefore win
By winging towards
The wisdom toothgaps of the canyon houses
LEGS AND BRAIN INTACT

ALAN SILLITOE

✑§ The Pardon

My dog lay dead five days without a grave
In the thick of summer, hid in a clump of pine
And a jungle of grass and honeysuckle-vine.
I who had loved him while he kept alive

Went only close enough to where he was
To sniff the heavy honeysuckle-smell
Twined with another odor heavier still
And hear the flies' intolerable buzz.

Well, I was ten and very much afraid.
In my kind world the dead were out of range
And I could not forgive the sad or strange
In beast or man. My father took the spade

And buried him. Last night I saw the grass
Slowly divide (it was the same scene
But now it glowed a fierce and mortal green)
And saw the dog emerging. I confess

I felt afraid again, but still he came
In the casual sun, clothed in a hymn of flies,
And death was breeding in his lively eyes.
I started in to cry and call his name,

Asking forgiveness of his tongueless head.
. . . I dreamt the past was never past redeeming:
But whether this was false or honest dreaming
I beg death's pardon now. And mourn the dead.

RICHARD WILBUR

There in the suddenly
   still
      wide street lay
Spot.

No dog so alone
   should
      ever have to mean
That—

Suddenly forever
   Still.

WILLIAM STAFFORD

The Survivor

We found the salmon on its side, the river no longer
Covering all of it, the hooked jaws gaping
And closing around as much sharp air as water.

It lay on the stones, far from the nesting hollow,
Its dark flanks battered cadaver-white, and fungus
Scaling its gills the color of marigolds.

"Help it," she said. "I can't help it, it's dying"—
Looking hard at the upper eye struck dull
As a stone, overcast with cataracts.

But it splashed to life, came scuttering, fishtailing
    forward
As if the two of us were a place upstream
And we saw its humpback writhe ashore, then tilt

Upright in an inch of water. It mouthed the ripples
And stared with both eyes now at the empty sunlight,
Not knowing where it was. I turned it away

With my boot, catching my breath. It lurched and slid
To a pool as deep as its body, then lunged in the
    current
And gradually fell downstream, while we followed it

(Where the yellow leaves came scattering to the shal-
    lows)
And watched its dorsal fin be joined by another
To hang there, wavering, for the cold time being.

DAVID WAGONER

ᥰᥩ Caring for Animals

I ask sometimes why these small animals
With bitter eyes, why we should care for them.

I question the sky, the serene blue water,
But it cannot say. It gives no answer.

And no answer releases in my head
A procession of grey shades patched and whimpering,

Dogs with clipped ears, wheezing cart horses
A fly without shadow and without thought.

Is it with these menaces to our vision
With this procession led by a man carrying wood

We must be concerned? The holy land, the rearing
Green island should be kindlier than this.

Yet the animals, our ghosts, need tending to.
Take in the whipped cat and the blinded owl;

Take up the man-trapped squirrel upon your shoulder.
Attend to the unnecessary beasts.

From growing mercy and a moderate love
Great love for the human animal occurs.

And your love grows. Your great love grows and
grows.

JON SILKIN

Sometimes running
to yes nothing and
too fast to look
where and at what
I stand and there
are trees sunning
themselves long a
brook going and
jays and jewelry
in all leafages
because I pause.

JOHN CIARDI

Once around a daisy counting
she loves me/she loves me not
and you're left with a golden
button without a petal left to
it. Don't count too much on
what you count on remaining
entirely a flower at the end.

JOHN CIARDI

❧ Who Are You, Little i

who are you, little i

(five or six years old)
peering from some high

window; at the gold

of november sunset

and feeling: that if day
has to become night

this is a beautiful way)

E. E. CUMMINGS

II

a ten-clawed monster

What makes us rove that starlit corridor
May be the impulse to meet face to face
Our vice and folly shaped into a thing,
And so at last ourselves; what lures us there
Is simpler versions of disaster:
A web that shuffles time and space,
A sentence to perpetual journeying,
A world of ocean without shore,
And simplest, flapping down the poisoned air,
A ten-clawed monster.

In him, perhaps, we see the general ogre
Who rode our ancestors to nightmare,
And in his habitat their maps of hell.
But climates and geographies soon change,
Spawning mutations none can quell
With silver sword or necromancer's ring,
Worse than their sires, of wider range,
And much more durable.

KINGSLEY AMIS

◄§ The Way I Hear It

Giving her mother a peck she picked
up the basket loaded with Girl Scout cookies,
zipped up her windbreaker to the hood and started
    down
that path winding so prettily from her house.

Chainsmoking in the wood he waited, his butts
littering the ground like snowdrops. It was,
he reflected, hard to be a wolf, with soft
nails and teeth no longer than the ordinary—

cold, baying at the moon fleeced white as snow,
running with that pack of shadows. He never
could explain the torn knees and elbows to his folks.
He put on his rubber Wolf Man's mask:

"Oh, cut it out, George!" she said, before
he could get out even an ordinary, slightly muted
growl. His claws hung long and pulpy at his side.
"I'll have to," he sighed, "work through Grandma!"

Grandma was tempted until she found
out he meant business, fled screaming to lock
herself in the bathroom and screw
her eye to the keyhole.

In bed, his moustache bristling over the coverlet,
he looked just like her: "Wow, Grandma, what a

heavy upper lip you have! Try the vanilla!" and Hood
was off to a forest ranger, in the vicinity

before she could hear his long rehearsed *Thebetter
totickleyouwithmydear!* Grandma yelped at
the keyhole, having swallowed the key. Rattling the
    door
she failed to hear the shot.

Skinned and hung up to dry he weighed 137
pounds, which is more than any other wolf
the ranger shot that season. They all noticed
his toes, short and stubby, the absence of a tail,

and called the papers. WOLF BOY! the papers
    screamed.
Mowgli leaped into the excited eyes of children
from the front page. *The Werewolf,* Hollywood
uttered another tired gasp. "Fifty-third nearly extinct

species!" the Sierra Club warned, but nobody listened,
except, perhaps, Red Riding Hood
who, drifting along the sidewalk, now hummed
a little, examining in a mirror white teeth, red lips.

ROBERT SIEGEL

✑ The Making of a Monster

*Found Poem: Poem found on Time Machine Toy
produced by the Mattel Corporation*

1 Put creature in Expansion Chamber
    until it is soft.
To see if it is soft,
        open Chamber door,
        poke creature with tongs.

When creature is soft, use tongs
        to put soft creature
        in Compressor.

2 WHEN CREATURE IS FULLY FORMED:
        Open Chamber door.
        Use tongs to take out space creature.

DO NOT USE YOUR FINGERS—

    CREATURE IS HOT!
        Let creature cool.

Now you can play with it.

ALBERT DRAKE

ఌ The Ballad of Ruby *

Her mother dressed the child in white,
White ribbons plaited in her hair,
And sent her off to school to fight
Though it was very cruel there.
"Ruby, we have to show our pride.
Walk slow, and just be dignified."

So Ruby walked to school each day
While the white mothers screamed "Black scum!"
Never got dirty out at play
For she spent recess in her room,
And felt the hatred seeping in.
"What is it, mother? What have I done?"

But still her mother had to trust
That that white dress so clean and neat
Would show the truth because it must,
Her Ruby was so bright and sweet.
And every day the crowd grew bigger
And threw stones at the "dirty nigger."

Then Ruby shook her ribboned head,
Refused to eat a chocolate cookie,
Had nightmares every night in bed,
Broke her brown crayons—"They are mucky!
"Ugly is black. Ugly is last."
(Ruby at six was learning fast).

* The story of Ruby is told by Robert Coles in *Children of Crisis,*
Atlantic Monthly Press, 1967.

And when the teacher let them draw,
Ruby made all black people lame,
White people tall, strong, without flaw.
Her drawing did not need a name.
"It is plain black and white, you see.
And black is ugly. Black is me."

"We'll poison you" became the taunt.
"You'll learn to keep away from white!"
And so a new fear came to haunt
The child who had no appetite,
Locked into blackness like some sin.
"Why mother? Is it *only* my skin?"

But still she walked to school with glory,
And ran the gauntlet, dignified. . . .
Did she grow up to tell a different story?—
"White folks are black, all dirty down inside.
What makes them like they are, ugly within?
Is it *only* the color of their skin?"

MAY SARTON

❧ Frankenstein by Mary W. Shelley

In his occult-science lab
Frankenstein creates a Flab
Which, endowed with human will,
Very shortly starts to kill.
First, it pleads a lonely life
And demands a monster-wife;
"Monstrous!" Frankenstein objects,
Thinking of the side-effects.

Chilled with fear, he quits the scene
But the frightful man-machine
Follows him in hot pursuit
Bumping people off *en route,*
Till at last it stands, malign,
By the corpse of Frankenstein!

Somewhere in the northern mists
—Horrid thing—*it still exists* ...
Still at large, a-thirst for gore!
Got a strong lock on your door?

MAURICE SAGOFF

✑ The Bride of Frankenstein

The Baron has decided to mate the monster,
to breed him perhaps,
in the interests of pure science, his only god.

So he goes up into his laboratory
which he has built in the tower of the castle
to be as near the interplanetary forces as possible,
and puts together the prettiest monster-woman you
    ever saw
with a body like a pin-up girl
and hardly any stitching at all
where he sewed on the head of a raped and murdered
    beauty queen.

He sets his liquids burping, and coils blinking and
    buzzing,
and waits for an electric storm to send through the
    equipment
the spark vital for life.
The storm breaks over the castle
and the equipment really goes crazy
like a kitchen full of modern appliances
as the lightning juice starts oozing right into that pretty
    corpse.

He goes to get the monster
so he will be right there when she opens her eyes,
for she might fall in love with the first thing she sees
as ducklings do.

That monster is already straining at his chains and
    slurping
ready to go right to it:
He has been well prepared for coupling
by his pinching leering keeper who's been saying for
weeks,
"You gonna get a little nookie, kid,"
or "How do you go for some poontang, baby."
All the evil in him is focused on this one thing now
as he is led into her very presence.

She awakens slowly,
she bats her eyes,
she gets up out of the equipment,
    and finally she stands in all her seamed glory,
a monster princess with a hairdo like a fright-wig,
lightning flashing in the background
like a halo and a wedding veil,
like a photographer snapping pictures of great
    moments.

She stands and stares with her electric eyes,
beginning to understand that in this life too
she was just another body to be raped.

The monster is ready to go:
He roars with joy at the sight of her,
so they let him loose and he goes right for those
    knockers.
And she starts screaming to break your heart
and you realize that she was just born:
In spite of her big tits she was just a baby.

But her instincts are right—
rather death than that green slobber:
She jumps off the parapet.
And then the monster's sex drive goes wild.
Thwarted, it turns to violence, demonstrating sublima-
    tion crudely,

and he wrecks the lab, those burping acids and buzzing
   coils,
overturning the control panel so the equipment goes
   off like a bomb,
the stone castle crumbling and crashing in the storm
destroying them all . . . perhaps.

Perhaps somehow the Baron got out of that wreckage
   of his dreams
with his evil intact if not his good looks
and more wicked than ever went on with his thrilling
   career.

And perhaps even the monster lived
to roam the earth, his desire still ungratified,
and lovers out walking in shadowy and deserted places
will see his shape loom up over them, their doom—
and children sleeping in their beds
will wake up in the dark night screaming
as his hideous body grabs them.

EDWARD FIELD

ᨔ 'B' Movie

Eyes glowing like headlights
   move through the trees
poking holes in darkness
   in search of you and me.

Where shall we hide? The last plane
   succumbs to black vines, its tires
eaten by ants. We send a radio message
   and the static snickers.

Clutching a little column of noon
   surrounded by spanish moss
we shiver in the violence of our sweat:
   flesh squeaks against flesh.

"Darling," I say to my shadow in your eye
   and point to the sawtooth mountains
where we may just escape the light
   that burns like acid.

The sun falls, a murdered grape.
   We hear only our echoes
gallop through the canyon,
   then far below

a dim signal
   followed by another.
Remote-controlled they come
   swaying sensitive apparatus.

We wake where robot faces
 lean in a circle above,
choosing surgical instruments.
 I ease out of one sleeve

and lunge at the lasar eye—
 glass—blue sparks—metal groans!
I grab you and crawl through the smoke.
 Incredibly, help comes.

*   *   *

Later, where the moon foams like lather
 on the wet cheek of the sand,
we two, new-pressed, clean-shaven,
 clinch . . . fade out . . . THE END.

ROBERT SIEGEL

Enter the dream-house, brothers and sisters, leaving
Your debts asleep, your history at the door:
This is the home for heroes, and this loving
Darkness a fur you can afford.

Fish in their tank electrically heated
Nose without envy the glass wall: for them
Clerk, spy, nurse, killer, prince, the great and the
    defeated,
Move in a mute day-dream.

Bathed in this common source, you gape incurious
At what your active hours have willed—
Sleep-walking on that silver wall, the furious
Sick shapes and pregnant fancies of your world.

There is the mayor opening the oyster season:
A society wedding: the autumn hats look swell:
An old crocks' race, and a politician
In fishing-waders to prove that all is well.

Oh, look at the warplanes! Screaming hysteric treble
In the long power-dive, like gannets they fall steep.
But what are they to trouble—
These silver shadows to trouble your watery, womb-
    deep sleep?

See the big guns, rising, groping, erected
To plant death in your world's soft womb.

Fire-bud, smoke-blossom, iron seed projected—
Are these exotics? They will grow nearer home:

Grow nearer home—and out of the dream-house
  stumbling
One night into a strangling air and the flung
Rags of children and thunder of stone niagaras
  tumbling,
You'll know you slept too long.

CECIL DAY LEWIS

✍§ The Man with the Ice Cream Cart

The man with the ice cream cart is near.
Children uncurling in their cramped rooms
hear his jingling row of little silver bells.
The man with the ice cream cart is near.
Dark flutes of my closed draperies
shut out the light; and I want to sleep.
But the man with the ice cream cart stops opposite
my windows, working his row of little silver bells.
The laughing children chase after him,
across the blanched gardens of my half-sleep.

I know him, though, for his true self—
at least his nights' self in starched white
wheeling a noiseless cart from bed to bed.
He stands now, by my own, dispensing the needed
    capsule.
If he were decked in bells from head to toe,
and I a child chasing after him, he would beckon
yet bog my every step in the mire
of all bad dreams, mocking my struggles on the muddy
    roads
of vain pursuit; then wake me in a sweat of fear,
plunging night forever through the heart of day.

FREDERICK NICKLAUS

❧ beware: do not read this poem

tonite, thriller was
abt an ol woman, so vain she
surrounded herself w/
    many mirrors

it got so bad that finally she
locked herself indoors & her
whole life became the
    mirrors

one day the villagers broke
into her house, but she was too
swift for them . she disappeared
    into a mirror
each tenant who bought the house
after that, lost a loved one to
    the ol woman in the mirror:
    first a little girl
    then a young woman
    then the young woman/s husband

the hunger of this poem is legendary
it has taken in many victims
back off from this poem
it has drawn in yr feet
back off from this poem
it has drawn in yr legs
back off from this poem
it is a greedy mirror

57

you are into this poem . from
    the waist down
nobody can hear you can they?
this poem has had you up to here
        belch
this poem ain't got no manners
you cant call out frm this poem
relax now & go w/this poem
move & roll on to this poem
do not resist this poem
this poem has yr eyes
this poem has his head
this poem has his arms
this poem has his fingers
this poem has his fingertips

this poem is the reader & the
reader this poem

statistic: the us bureau of missing persons reports
        that in 1968 over 100,000 people disappeared
        leaving no solid clues
            nor trace   only
a space   in the lives of their friends

                                        ISHMAEL REED

III

---

in twos and threes they
whisper past my house

ᵉᵍ Dream of the Black Mother

To My Mother

Black mother
Rocks her son
And in her black head
Covered with black hair
She keeps marvellous dreams.

Black mother
Rocks her son
And forgets
That the earth has dried up the maize
That yesterday the groundnuts were finished.

She dreams of marvellous worlds
Where her son would go to school
To school where men study.

Black mother
Rocks her son
And forgets
Her brothers building towns and cities
Cementing them with their blood.

She dreams of marvellous worlds
Where her son would run along the street
The street where men pass by.

Black mother
Rocks her son
And listening
To the voice from afar
Brought by the wind.

She dreams of marvellous worlds,
Marvellous worlds
Where her son will be able to live.

KALUNGANO

❧ The Writer

In her room at the prow of the house
Where light breaks, and the windows are tossed with
    linden,
My daughter is writing a story.

I pause in the stairwell, hearing
From her shut door a commotion of typewriter-keys
Like a chain hauled over a gunwale.

Young as she is, the stuff
Of her life is a great cargo, and some of it heavy:
I wish her a lucky passage.

But now it is she who pauses,
As if to reject my thought and its easy figure.
A stillness greatens, in which

The whole house seems to be thinking,
And then she is at it again with a bunched clamor
Of strokes, and again is silent.

I remember the dazed starling
Which was trapped in that very room, two years ago;
How we stole in, lifted a sash

And retreated, not to affright it;
And how for a helpless hour, through the crack of the
    door,
We watched the sleek, wild, dark

And iridescent creature
Batter against the brilliance, drop like a glove
To the hard floor, or the desk-top,
And wait then, humped and bloody,
For the wits to try it again; and how our spirits
Rose when, suddenly sure,

It lifted off from a chair-back,
Beating a smooth course for the right window
And clearing the sill of the world.

It is always a matter, my darling,
Of life or death, as I had forgotten I wish
What I wished you before, but harder.

RICHARD WILBUR

✑ Nancy

Trying hard to look hard,
You balance with one ankle turning under,
Your eyes, sloping off your face,
Wanting only the chosen word overheard.

I wonder at your clothes:
The expensive skirt,
The leather boots,
Clinging to your calves,
Plinths for thighs from sculpture.

Hearing the little moan
Behind your voice,
The little tug that signals:
"I am communicating with the enemy."

I wait with prideful patience,
For I have heard you after every class—
What is it? Twenty times this term?
And each time my patience seems more marvelous to
   me.

Speaking of relevance, explaining where I went wrong,
Showing me the existential skull
Beneath my skin-deep philosophy,
Wanting me only to know that I have failed you,
Have driven you to the barricades.

My mind wanders among your threats of anarchy,
Blood in the streets. The tenacity of you!
Every day sullen; every day burning
With borrowed fire.

Are we making love, you and I,
Across this fumed-oak desk?
You who would bridge the generation gap
With human chains of the immolated underprivileged.

In the faculty meeting, someone rose, saying:
Ladies and gentlemen, we are confronted with
The first generation that was picked up
Everytime it cried.

And from this tyranny of solicitude
I send you back, beloved,
To the barricades
In your expensive skirt.

RICHARD PECK

The Party

They served tea in the sandpile, together with
Mudpies baked on the sidewalk.
After tea
The youngest said that he had had a good dinner,
The oldest dressed for a dance,
And they sallied forth together with water pots
To moisten a rusted fire truck on account of it
Might rain.

I watched from my study,
Thought of my part in these contributions to world
Gaiety, and resolved
That the very least acknowledgment I could make
Would be to join them;
               so we
All took our watering pots (filled with pies)
And poured tea on our dog. Then I kissed the children
And told them that when they grew up we would have
Real tea parties.
"That did be fun!" the youngest shouted, and ate pies
With wild surmise.

REED WHITTEMORE

Judy

You have the light step
of Ariel, the smile of Puck,
something of Rosalind's
courage, I think, though you are small
as I imagine Perdita to have been

(and why Shakespeare gets into all this at all
I don't know—but he does, insistently)

but when you set off alone, winter nights,
coat collar up, and in your pocket
that invisible flute,

it's myself I think of, 12 years old
trudging home from the library lugging
too many books, and seeing

visions in Ilford High Road,

the passing faces oblivious
to all their own strange beauty under the street-lamps,

and I drunk on it.

DENISE LEVERTOV

"It Out-Herods Herod, Pray You Avoid It"

Tonight my children hunch
Toward their Western, and are glad
As, with a Sunday punch,
The Good casts out the Bad.

And in their fairy tales
The warty giant and witch
Get sealed in doorless jails
And the match-girl strikes it rich.

I've made myself a drink.
The giant and witch are set
To bust out of the clink
When my children have gone to bed.

For the wicked have grown strong,
Their numbers mock at death,
Their cow brings forth its young,
Their bull engendereth.

Their very fund of strength,
Satan, bestrides the globe;
He stalks its breadth and length
And finds out even Job.

Yet by quite other laws
My children make their cause;

Half God, half Santa Claus,
But with my voice and face,

A hero comes to save
The poorman, beggarman, thief,
And make the world behave
And put an end to grief.

And that their sleep be sound
I say this childermas
Who could not, at one time,
Have saved them from the gas.

ANTHONY HECHT

Miss Foster

I see the schoolbus let them off at school
like some brightly colored mechanical sow
casting her litter patiently under the trees

or Noah's Ark on wheels. Free, they run
scuffing a white glitter from the grass,
their voices a thinning circle of sharp sound.

Noon stretches out on the enameled hull.
Leaves swim thin and dusty in the light
blazing like Lucifer on the windshield.

Wheeling to the cool side of the porch,
where aphids' milk makes the railing tacky,
I sleep with locusts singing in the garden.

Later as the sun narrows to a coal
floating in each of the bus's seven windows,
their laughter snags me like the shriek of chalk.

In twos and threes they whisper past my house
to clatter up the iron-stippled stair
as darkness floods the world. With a small sigh

steel doors swallow the last pair.

ROBERT SIEGEL

✺ On My Child's Death
(Auf Meines Kindes Tod [8])

Clocks strike in the distance,
Already the night grows late,
How dimly the lamp glistens;
Your bed is all made.

It is the wind goes, only,
Grieving around the house;
Where, inside, we sit lonely
Often listening out.

It is as if, how lightly,
You must be going to knock,
Had missed your way and might be
Tired, now, coming back.

We are poor, poor stupid folk!
It's we, still lost in dread,
Who wander in the dark—
You've long since found your bed.

JOSEPH VON EICHENDORFF

IV

the houses that our fathers built

Time and the weather wear away
The houses that our fathers built.
Their ghostly furniture remains:
All the sad sofas we have stained
With tears of boredom and of guilt,

The fraying mottoes, the stopped clocks . . .
And still sometimes these tired shapes
Taunt the damp parlors of the heart.
What Sunday prisons they recall!
And what miraculous escapes!

DONALD JUSTICE

One pale goldfish patrols the globe on Teacher's desk
goggles the charmed room, the blackboard's calm
assertion—the X2's. A book on the chalktray
hitches itself up like a puppy with one leg
out of its basket; a tennis shoe seeks its
tongue—a culprit—from the closet; overhead
the watercolors of Halloween wait for Thanksgiving.

A window blind blinks at "Now is the time for all
good men," and a greater truth flourishes on the wall:
"The quick brown fox." The pale goldfish learns it
all by rote; his intermittent eye pans gigantic
lessons all day long, then the night's
curriculum: blackboard, streetlight, stars.

WILLIAM STAFFORD

Mother was a crack of light
And a gray eye peeping;
I made believe by breathing hard
That I was sleeping.

Sister's doughboy on last leave
Had robbed me of her hand;
Downstairs at intervals she played
Warum on the baby grand.

Under the roof a wardrobe trunk
Whose lock a boy could pick
Contained a red Masonic hat
And a walking stick.

Bolt upright in my bed that night
I saw my father flying.
The wind was walking on my neck,
The window-panes were crying.

STANLEY KUNITZ

⋞ Three Blocks West, On Sunday

It's not what your mother used to do
    on Sundays after the chicken and ice cream,
      staggering down desolate streets.
You're lucky to have your stuffed chicken and
    stomach and chair and that's enough,
      and no knowledge of. You're lucky maybe.
This is not what you see:
Sundays, three blocks west.

Youth with a stick of kindling playing
    baseball with thin boys, crying
      words (which we shall not print here
        or anywhere for that matter(between
condemned tenements
    (but inhabited,
      by people and rats)
        whose doors boarded up
          will make more baseball slats and firewood.
Surprisingly faces look out of missing glass:
black face (of a thin black boy watching thin white
    boys playing baseball)
    stares from a blank black square,
      white face of woman opens at an upstairs
      aperture
      its mouth and calls,
and a small fluffy dog scrubbed clean
    (by someone) runs next door into empty cellar
    space

beamed over by supports where a burnt-out
house had been.
The barbershop has also stars-and-stripes in the
showcase
and last summer's flypaper; it isn't pretty
but an old man
stands, looks, and does not move from this
display,
talking, talking to no one. This is the end of the city.
Here people dwindle to no people; railroad tracks
are last. The boys who wanted to run away
came, and some of them jumped the freights, and some
of those (you know)—

You were well brought up by mothers; what do you
see?
What do you see from the window on peaceful
Sundays,
when you rise from newspaper sheets
and stretch (remembering the chicken) and look twenty
stories to the street?

Why, the people look like flies!
Who could imagine it?
It's a wonderful view of the city.

LENORE MARSHALL

৺ Fourteenth Birthday

The Enemy, who wears
Her mother's usual face
And confidential tone,
Has access; doubtless stares
Into her writing case
And listens on the phone.

Her fortress crumbles. Spies
Who call themselves her betters
Harry her night and day.
Herself's the single prize.
Likely they read her letters
And bear the tale away,

Or eavesdrop on her sleep
(Uncountered and unchidden)
To learn her dreams by heart.
There is no lock will keep
A secret rightly hidden
From their subversive art.

But till the end is sure,
Till on some open plain
They bring her to her knees,
She'll face them down—endure
In silence and disdain
Love's utmost treacheries.

PHYLLIS McGINLEY

My distant cousin,
I don't think I noticed you. I was
Too busy listening to the grown-up
Conversations. Then you asked
If I would enlist in your imaginary
Army.

I   remember you
Asking me to lie down
On the big red sofa in my
Grandmother's living room. I was
Seven and obedient. You
Asked to remove my socks. My
Shoes. My skirt. You tried
To unfasten my small white
Peter Pan collar. "Don't do that,"
I whispered,
"Or I will go tell my mother."

The living
Room.

I understood
Sea shells. The noise of tears. You
Wanted to be a man in that place
Of objets d'art and windows, where everything
In grown-up lives had gone wrong.

You believed in your body. That small
Boy body with a certainty of its own.
You knew, and I knew, we could be set
Free by our arms.

SANDRA HOCHMAN

❧ The Pet Shop

I never had the luck to keep a pet:
canary, rabbit, kitten, all were tried,
When she went mad, my father drowned the cat;
the rabbit fretted, the canaries died.

So, though my legs grew longer than my years,
I had no pup to race me round the hills.
The very sticklebacks brought home in jars,
within the weeks, were furred with fishy ills.

But when, on Saturdays, we went to town,
my chums and I, one window drew our gaze:
glass-tanks of snakes and lizards green and brown;
white mice and piebald mice on sawdust trays;
dumb tortoises; a haughty cockatoo;
bright-feathered bantams picking in the grit;
quick ferrets sniffing straw for something new,
and pigeons jerking on pink, clockwork feet.

Among the crowd that idled round the door,
you'd sometimes see a fellow slip his hand
into a hidden pocket to withdraw
a cowering lark or linnet contraband.

JOHN HEWITT

This sad house.
Two girls gone.
The third girl

left, fifteen.
Three years to
go. Late from

staying after
school, she eats
alone with both

the same old
parents. Same
old meal: they

drink, she eats;
they eat, she
clears her plate.

Lead questions.
Moral mouth-
fuls. Between

them she grows
old, she tells
the same old

lies. Her sisters
have abandoned
her; she's wiser

than an only
child. She chokes
on what they

all three know,
meal after
meal: the house

is sad, it
cannot
hold.

PHILIP BOOTH

⇜ The Wise Child

I couldn't wait. My childhood angered me.
It was a sickness time would cure in time,
But clocks were doctors slow to make me well.
I sulked and raged. My parents told me "play"—
I stood in the garden shouting my own name.
The noise enlarged me. I can hear it still.

At last I've come where then I longed to go.
And what's the change?—I find that I can choose
To wish for where I started. Childhood puts
Its prettiest manners on. I see the dew
Filming the lawn I stamped.
                    The wise child knows
Not here, not there, the perfect somewhere waits.

EDWARD LUCIE-SMITH

Robin Hood
When I was twelve,
In your greenwood
How I would selve
Myself, rob rich
Legend to give
Poor everyday.
With you I'd rive
The willow-switch
And our sword-play
Left Gisbourne in
A bestial skin.
And with you, hale
At the Blue Boar Inn,
I drank brown ale,
Clanked nipperkin
With Allan-a-Dale,
Took Stutely from
His gallows-cart,
Saw Sheriff pale
And King smart
When finger and thumb,
Unmatched, would loose
Clothyard shaft
And the grey goose
Feather flew
And arrow sang
A song more true
Than art or craft
Or history knew.

GRAY BURR

When I was little, oh a very small boy,
With a Ford, fish, and go fly your kite,
I lived in a house in a cookie jar joy,
With a bed, game, and I'm it tonight.

I wore short pants and had dimples in my knees,
With a Whitney-Pratt, call me that again.
I had a girl friend more pretty than you please,
With a top, bee, and so's your old man.

I played in the street, oh I never saw school,
With a Campbell can, and knock *that* off,
I hid and I sought and I broke THE rule,
With a me, who, and why don't you cough?

When I was happy, oh a very small boy,
With a sink, stove, and jump in the lake,
I made mud huts I would never destroy,
With a strap, please, be good for my sake.

I didn't grow much, and then I grew fast,
With a book, bat, and why don't you try?
I never was first but I was never last,
With a good, bad, and who knows why?

I grew like grass, Oh! we said, Like corn!
With an ache, break, and which way to go?
I dreamed some nights that I'd never been born,
With a glad, sad—I still don't know.

ANTHONY OSTROFF

V

touch me if you can

☙ Corner

The cop slumps alertly on his motorcycle,
Supported by one leg like a leather stork.
His glance accuses me of loitering.
I can see his eyes moving like fish
In the green depths of his green goggles.

His ease is fake. I can tell.
My ease is fake. And he can tell.
The fingers armored by his gloves
Splay and clench, itching to change something.
As if he were my enemy or my death,
I just stand there watching.

I spit out my gum which has gone stale.
I knock out a new cigarette—
Which is my bravery.
It is all imperceptible:
The way I shift my weight,
The way he creaks in his saddle.

The traffic is specific though constant.
The sun surrounds me, divides the street between us.
His crash helmet is whiter in the shade.
It is like a bull ring as they say it is just before the
    fighting.
I cannot back down. I am there.
Everything holds me back.
I am in danger of disappearing into the sunny dust.
My levis bake and my T shirt sweats.

My cigarette makes my eyes burn.
But I don't dare drop it.

Who made him my enemy?
Prince of coolness. King of fear.
Why do I lean here waiting?
Why does he lounge there watching?

I am becoming sunlight.
My hair is on fire. My boots run like tar.
I am hung-up by the bright air.

Something breaks through all of a sudden,
And he blasts off, quick as a craver,
Smug in his power; watching me watch.

RALPH POMEROY

✒§ Miriam

Her long legs stepped across the furniture
And into another world. There stood
A tall girl stepping over furniture
And into another world. Was she
The movie she was watching? Or was she
The girl she watched, watching the movie?
Either way it was "The Miriam Story"
Played by Miriam who was writing the story
Of Miriam playing "The Miriam Story."

The dialogue should have gone like this,
The monologue ("I mean.") should have gone like this:

"If you accept me, I will turn away.
If you reject me, I will turn toward you.
I feel so much. Touch me if you can.
And, oh, if I say no, please try again."

HOWARD MOSS

~§ Cousin Nancy

Miss Nancy Ellicott
Strode across the hills and broke them,
Rode across the hills and broke them—
The barren New England hills—
Riding to hounds
Over the cow-pasture.

  Miss Nancy Ellicott smoked
And danced all the modern dances;
And her aunts were not quite sure how they felt about
    it,
But they knew it was modern.

  Upon the glazen shelves kept watch
Matthew and Waldo, guardians of the faith,
The army of unalterable law.

T. S. ELIOT

❧ The Lonely Street

School is over. It is too hot
to walk at ease. At ease
in light frocks they walk the streets
to while the time away.
They have grown tall. They hold
pink flames in their right hands.
In white from head to foot,
with sidelong, idle look—
in yellow, floating stuff,
black sash and stockings—
touching their avid mouths
with pink sugar on a stick—
like a carnation each holds in her hand—
they mount the lonely street.

WILLIAM CARLOS WILLIAMS

❧ An Elementary School Classroom
in a Slum

Far far from gusty waves these children's faces.
Like rootless weeds the torn hair round their paleness.
The tall girl with her weighed-down head. The paper-
Seeming boy with rat's eyes. The stunted unlucky heir
Of twisted bones, reciting a father's gnarled disease,
His lesson from his desk. At back of the dim class
One unnoted, mild and young: his eyes live in a dream
Of squirrels' game, in tree room, other than this.

On sour cream walls, donations. Shakespeare's head
Cloudless at dawn, civilized dome riding all cities.
Belled, flowery, Tyrolese valley. Open-handed map
Awarding the world its world. And yet, for these
Children, these windows, not this world, are world,
Where all their future's painted with a fog,
A narrow street sealed in with a lead sky,
Far far from rivers, capes, and stars of words.

Surely Shakespeare is wicked, the map a bad example
With ship and sun and love tempting them to steal—
For lives that slyly turn in their cramped holes
From fog to endless night? On their slag heap, these
    children
Wear skins peeped through by bones, and spectacles of
    steel
With mended glass, like bottle bits in slag.
Tyrol is wicked; map's promising a fable:

All of their time and space are foggy slum,
So blot their maps with slums as big as doom.

Unless, governor, teacher, inspector, visitor,
This map becomes their window and these windows
That open on their lives like crouching tombs
Break, O break open, till they break the town
And show the children to the fields and all their world
Azure on their sands, to let their tongues
Run naked into books, the white and green leaves open
The history theirs whose language is the sun.

STEPHEN SPENDER

On Driving Behind A School Bus For Mentally Retarded Children

Full deep green
bloom-fallen spring
here outside,
for us.

They,
like winter-covered crocuses:
strange bright beauty
peeping through snow
that never melts—

(How quietly,
how quietly,
the bus.)

These flowers have no fragrance.
They move to an eerie wind
I cannot feel.
They rise, with petals fully opened,
from a twisted seed,
and neither grow
nor wither.

They will be taught
the colors of their names.

GRACE BUTCHER

✑ Cherrylog Road

Off Highway 106
At Cherrylog Road, I entered
The '34 Ford without wheels,
Smothered in kudzu,
With a seat pulled out to run
Corn whiskey down from the hills,

And then, from the other side,
Crept into an Essex
With a rumble seat of red leather,
And then, out again, aboard
A blue Chevrolet, releasing
The rust from its other color,

Reared up on three building blocks.
None had the same body heat;
I changed with them inward, toward
The weedy heart of the junk yard,
For I knew that Charlotte Holbrook
Would escape from her father at noon

And would come from the farm
To seek parts owned by the sun
Among the abandoned chassis,
Sitting in each in turn
As I did, leaning forward,
As in a wild stock-car race

In the parking lot of the dead.
Time after time, I climbed in
And out the other side, like
An envoy or movie star
Met at the station by crickets.
A radiator cap raised its head,

Became a real toad or a kingsnake,
As I neared the hub of the yard,
Passing through many states,
Many lives, to reach
Some grandmother's long Pierce-Arrow
Sending platters of blindness forth

From its nickel hubcaps
And spilling its tender upholstery
On sleepy roaches,
The glass panel in between
Lady and colored driver
Not all the way broken out,

The back-seat phone
Still on its hook.
I got in as though to exclaim,
"Let us go to the orphan asylum,
John; I have some old toys
For children who say their prayers."

I popped with sweat as I thought
I heard Charlotte Holbrook scrape
Like a mouse in the Southern-state sun
That was eating the paint in blisters
From a hundred car tops and hoods.
She was tapping like code,

Loosening the screws,
Carrying off headlights,
Sparkplugs, bumpers,

Cracked mirrors and gear knobs,
Getting ready, already,
To go back with something to show

Other than her lips' new trembling
I would hold to me soon, soon,
Where I sat in the ripped back seat
Talking over the interphone,
Praying for Charlotte Holbrook
To come from her father's farm

And to get back there
With no trace of me on her face
To be seen by her red-haired father,
Who would change, in the squalling barn,
Her back's pale skin with a strop,
Then lay for me

In a bootlegger's roasting car
With a string-triggered 12-gauge shotgun
To blast the breath from the air.
Not cut by the jagged windshields,
Through the acres of wrecks she came,
With a wrench in her hand,

Through dust where the blacksnake dies
Of boredom, and the beetle knows
The compost has no more life.
Someone outside would have seen
The oldest car's door inexplicably
Close from within.

I held her and held her and held her,
Convoyed at terrific speed
By the stalled, dreaming traffic around us,
So the blacksnake, stiff
With inaction, curved back
Into life, and hunted the mouse

With deadly overexcitement,
The beetles reclaimed their field
As we clung, glued together,
With the hooks of the seat springs
Working through to catch us red-handed
Amidst the gray, breathless batting

That burst from the seat at our backs.
We left by separate doors
Into the changed, other bodies
Of cars, she down Cherrylog Road,
And I to my motorcycle,
Parked like the soul of the junk yard

Restored, a bicycle fleshed
With power, and tore off
Up Highway 106, continually
Drunk on the wind in my mouth,
Wringing the handlebars for speed,
Wild to be wreckage forever.

JAMES DICKEY

I do remember an apothecary,
And hereabouts 'a dwells

It baffles the foreigner like an idiom,
And he is right to adopt it as a form
Less serious than the living-room or bar;
    For it disestablishes the cafe,
Is a collective, and on basic country.

Not that it praises hygiene and corrupts
The ice-cream parlor and the tobacconist's
Is it a center; but that the attractive symbols
    Watch over puberty and leer
Like rubber bottles waiting for sick-use.

Youth comes to jingle nickels and crack wise;
The baseball scores are his, the magazines
Devoted to lust, the jazz, the Coca-Cola,
    The lending-library of love's latest.
He is the customer; he is heroized.

And every nook and cranny of the flesh
Is spoken to by packages with wiles.
"Buy me, buy me," they whimper and cajole;
    The hectic range of lipsticks pouts,
Revealing the wicked and the simple mouth.

With scarcely any evasion in their eye
They smoke, undress their girls, exact a stance;
But only for a moment. The clock goes round;
    Crude fellowships are made and lost;
They slump in booths like rags, not even drunk.

KARL SHAPIRO

Next year the grave grass will cover us.
We stand now, and laugh;
Watching the girls go by;
Betting on slow horses; drinking cheap gin.
We have nothing to do; nowhere to go; nobody.

Last year was a year ago; nothing more.
We weren't younger then; nor older now.

We manage to have the look that young men have;
We feel nothing behind our faces, one way or other.

We shall probably not be quite dead when we die.
We were never anything all the way; not even soldiers.

We are the insulted, brother, the desolate boys.
Sleepwalkers in a dark and terrible land,
Where solitude is a dirty knife at our throats.
Cold stars watch us, chum,
Cold stars and the whores.

KENNETH PATCHEN

Values In Use

I attended school and I liked the place—
grass and little locust-leaf shadows like lace.

Writing was discussed. They said, "We create
values in the process of living, daren't await

their historic progress." Be abstract
and you'll wish you'd been specific; it's a fact.

What was I studying? Values in use,
"judged on their own ground." Am I still abstruse?

Walking along, a student said offhand,
" 'Relevant' and 'plausible' were words I understand."

A pleasing statement, anonymous friend.
Certainly the means must not defeat the end.

MARIANNE MOORE

VI

it is sometimes summer

Oysters we ate,
sweet blue babies,
twelve eyes looked up at me,
running with lemon and Tabasco.
I was afraid to eat this father-food
and Father laughed
and drank down his martini,
clear as tears.
It was a soft medicine
that came from the sea into my mouth,
moist and plump.
I swallowed.
It went down like a large pudding.
Then I ate one o'clock and two o'clock.
Then I laughed and then we laughed
and let me take note—
there was a death,
the death of childhood
there at the Union Oyster House
for I was fifteen
and eating oysters
and the child was defeated.
The woman won.

ANNE SEXTON

♪ Men at Forty

Men at forty
Learn to close softly
The doors to rooms they will not be
Coming back to.

At rest on a stair landing,
They feel it moving
Beneath them now like the deck of a ship,
Though the swell is gentle.

And deep in mirrors
They rediscover
The face of the boy as he practices tying
His father's tie there in secret

And the face of that father,
Still warm with the mystery of lather.
They are more fathers than sons themselves now.
Something is filling them, something

This is like the twilight sound
Of the crickets, immense,
Filling the woods at the foot of the slope
Behind their mortgaged homes.

DONALD JUSTICE

❧ On the Wagon

In between drinks I go on the wagon
which is sometimes a sleigh
and always filled with children,
including me,
the ears of horses like furred leaves,
the reins black over rumps
that resemble gray, cleft apples,
the smell of leather strong as brown medicine.

It is sometimes summer
and my cousin and I
actually ride the horses
and feel their backs—
broad, alive, and separate—
under our legs
thrust out, spraddled,
like short tan oars.

Sometimes there is hay in the box,
and that is a weed-sweet, wild-smell,
hot-heady bundle
of what was rooted, clovered, seasoned,
and sickled into a great, riding pillow
where we can roll under the passing sky.

It is at other times winter
and the smoke of the horses
is like the breath of fires,

and if I could, even now,
I would sneak inside,
stow away and lean against those hearts
stroking above every kind of ice and sweat
and desire.

ADRIEN STOUTENBURG

o by the by
has anybody seen
little you-i
who stood on a green
hill and threw
his wish at blue

with a swoop and a dart
out flew his wish
(it dived like a fish
but it climbed like a dream)
throbbing like a heart
singing like a flame

blue took it my
far beyond far
and high beyond high
bluer took it your
but bluest took it our
away beyond where

what a wonderful thing
is the end of a string
(murmurs little you-i
as the hill becomes nil)
and will somebody tell
me why people let go.

E. E. CUMMINGS

112

੪ Child on Top of a Greenhouse

The wind billowing out the seat of my britches,
My feet crackling splinters of glass and dried putty,
The half-grown chrysanthemums staring up like
   accusers
Up through the streaked glass, flashing with sunlight,
A few white clouds all rushing eastward,
A line of elms plunging and tossing like horses,
And everyone, everyone pointing up and shouting!

THEODORE ROETHKE

✑ First Song

Then it was dusk in Illinois, the small boy
After an afternoon of carting dung
Hung on the rail fence, a sapped thing
Weary to crying. Dark was growing tall
And he began to hear the pond frogs all
Calling upon his ear with what seemed their joy.

Soon their sound was pleasant for a boy
Listening in the smoky dusk and the nightfall
Of Illinois, and then from the field two small
Boys came bearing cornstalk violins
And rubbed three cornstalk bows with resins,
And they set fiddling with them as with joy.

It was now fine music the frogs and the boys
Did in the towering Illinois twilight make
And into dark in spite of a right arm's ache
A boy's hunched body loved out of a stalk
The first song of his happiness, and the song woke
His heart to the darkness and into the sadness of joy.

GALWAY KINNELL

When I see birches bend to left and right
Across the lines of straighter darker trees,
I like to think some boy's been swinging them.
But swinging doesn't bend them down to stay.
Ice-storms do that. Often you must have seen them
Loaded with ice a sunny winter morning
After a rain. They click upon themselves
As the breeze rises, and turn many-colored
As the stir cracks and crazes their enamel.
Soon the sun's warmth makes them shed crystal shells
Shattering and avalanching on the snow-crust—
Such heaps of broken glass to sweep away
You'd think the inner dome of heaven had fallen.
They are dragged to the withered bracken by the load,
And they seem not to break; though once they are
   bowed
So low for long, they never right themselves:
You may see their trunks arching in the woods
Years afterward, trailing their leaves on the ground
Like girls on hands and knees that throw their hair
Before them over their heads to dry in the sun.
But I was going to say when Truth broke in
With all her matter-of-fact about the ice-storm
I should prefer to have some boy bend them
As he went out and in to fetch the cows—
Some boy too far from town to learn baseball,
Whose only play was what he found himself,
Summer or winter, and could play alone,
One by one he subdued his father's trees

By riding them down over and over again
Until he took the stiffness out of them,
And not one but hung limp, not one was left
For him to conquer. He learned all there was
To learn about not launching out too soon
And so not carrying the tree away
Clear to the ground. He always kept his poise
To the top branches, climbing carefully
With the same pains you use to fill a cup
Up to the brim, and even above the brim.
Then he flung outward, feet first, with a swish,
Kicking his way down through the air to the ground.
So was I once a swinger of birches.
And so I dream of going back to be.
It's when I'm weary of considerations,
And life is too much like a pathless wood
Where your face burns and tickles with the cobwebs
Broken across it, and one eye is weeping
From a twig's having lashed across it open.
I'd like to get away from earth awhile
And then come back to it and begin over.
May no fate willfully misunderstand me
And half grant what I wish and snatch me away
Not to return. Earth's the right place for love;
I don't know where it's likely to go better.
I'd like to go by climbing a birch tree,
And climb black branches up a snow-white trunk
Toward heaven, till the tree could bear no more,
But dipped its top and set me down again.
That would be good both going and coming back.
One could do worse than be a swinger of birches.

ROBERT FROST

All the Fancy Things

music and painting and all that
That's all they thought of
in Puerto Rico in the old Spanish
days when she was a girl

So that now
she doesn't know what to do
with herself alone
and growing old up here—

Green is green
but the tag ends
of older things, *ma chere*

must withstand rebuffs
from that which returns
to the beginnings—

Or what? a
clean air, high up, unoffended
by gross odors.

WILLIAM CARLOS WILLIAMS

ଏ§ Palm Leaves of Childhood

When I was very small indeed,
and Joe and Fred were six-year giants,
my father, they and I, with soil
did mix farm-yard manure.
In this we planted coconuts,
naming them by brothers' names.
The palms grew faster far than I;
they, flowering, reached their goal!
Like the ear-rings that my sisters wore
came the tender golden flowers.
I watched them grow from gold to green;
then nuts as large as Tata's head.
I craved the milk I knew they bore.
I listened to the whispering leaves:
to the chattering, rattling, whispering leaves,
when night winds did wake.
They haunt me still in work and play:
those whispering leaves behind the slit
on the cabin wall of childhood's
dreaming and becoming.

G. ADALI-MORTTI

Babe Ruth

While Babe Ruth hit those homers I was a kid
Staggering up to the plate in my own bold stance:
Smile, feet wide, swinging the way he did,
Swaggering Babe, whose shoulders leapt in a dance.
June, when a diamond glittered the vacant lot,
Gang with me, bare feet or spikes, too scared to spit:
Noon, the ninth, I'm up, hearing the hot
Clang of the crowd yelling—*Hit, kid, hit!*

Pitch—a pop fly to short—I throw my bat,
Smugger than ever, playing the crowd, salt
Itch of the sweat of shame on my hands. I spat.
Fanning the air, now, on another bench,
Slugger gone sluggish, my hands in their love's fault,
Planning no pride, merely clench and unclench.

PAUL ENGLE

✎⌇ Nikki-Rosa

childhood remembrances are always a drag
if you're Black
you always remember things like living in Woodlawn
with no inside toilet
and if you become famous or something
they never talk about how happy you were to have
your mother
all to yourself and
how good the water felt when you got your bath
from one of those
big tubs that folk in chicago barbecue in
and somehow when you talk about home
it never gets across how much you
understood their feelings
as the whole family attended meetings about Hollydale
and even though you remember
your biographers never understand
your father's pain as he sells his stock
and another dream goes
And though you're poor it isn't poverty that
concerns you
and though they fought a lot
it isn't your father's drinking that makes any difference
but only that everybody is together and you
and your sister have happy birthdays and very good
Christmasses
and I really hope no white person ever has cause
to write about me

because they never understand
Black love is Black wealth and they'll
probably talk about my hard childhood
and never understand that
all the while I was quite happy

NIKKI GIOVANNI

On the Death of Friends in Childhood

We shall not ever meet them bearded in heaven,
Nor sunning themselves among the bald of hell;
If anywhere, in the deserted schoolyard at twilight,
Forming a ring, perhaps, or joining hands
In games whose very names we have forgotten.
Come, memory, let us seek them there in the shadows.

DONALD JUSTICE

ᵉ§ Old Age Blues

What are those children so happy about?
You would think they knew,
But none of them does,
How the world no longer is what it was.

The blood has drained from most of its heart.
Only this part—
Those children there—
What can they be so blithe about?

Tell them, please, to be still, and wait.
It is getting late,
And the dark comes down.
This world will never be what it was.

MARK VAN DOREN

VII

---

under your permanent skin

✑ Before the Coming of Winter

I counted the shapes
of my face on the dying
leaves

& was never cheated

Choose my body too
empty the trees
onto their shadows

I want to be lean & tough
as a fir
& float across the snow
in green
like an enormous flame

DENNIS SCHMITZ

If, as well may happen,
 On an autumn day
When white clouds go scudding
 And winds are gay,

Some earth-bound spirit
 A man lately dead,
(Your fellow-clerk) should take it
 Into his crazed head

To adopt a more venturesome
 Shape than a dead leaf
And wish you a 'good morning'
 Abrupt and brief,

He will come disguised
 As a sheet of newspaper
Charging across the square
 With a clumsy caper,

To flatten himself out
 Across your shins and knees
In a supplant posture:
 'Read me, please!'

Then scanning every column
 On both sides, with care,
You will find that clerk's name
 Printed somewhere—

Unless, perhaps, in warning
  The sheet comes blown
And the name which you stumble on
  Is, alas, your own.

ROBERT GRAVES

✑ Song for the Make-Up Man

The make-up man
Is full of faces
He comes to you sweetly
With pink for your ears

Lean back and smile
He will change your face
His colors all cover
Your wrinkles your fears

In a time of thunder
And nowhere to turn
He comes to your sleep
His fingers begin

Forehead to chin
Ear across to ear
Shadow for the eyes
You're a different man

But who knows what terror
Clings to you then
Cringing under
Your permanent skin

Did you ever see
Such a hiding of possessions
Did you ever see
Such a washing of sins

NORMAN ROSTEN

ᴥ The Clown

Aloof, reserved, yet strangely vulnerable,
Making of art a nonchalance, mere skill

As though a skill were something not to care
Too much about. You throw balls in the air,

You make yourself ridiculous, your face
Fitting nowhere but in a taut white space.

Yet sometimes carelessly you have been drawn
By painters in their note-book moments when

A special grace appears but fits nowhere—
A harlequin who leans upon a chair,

A youth who idly strums an old guitar,
Each lazy gesture meaning 'I don't care'.

ELIZABETH JENNINGS

✑ Frogman

1   Unsettling silt
In the holds of liners,

Nudging about
Under greasy piers, wrench,

File and crowbar
Remotely in contact,

Cantilevers
Coming and going on

The strength of bolts
He had better locate—

He bargained for
All that. It was a job.

2   Now after hours
In the dirtiest reach

He tries old tyres,
Petrol drums, carcasses

And pokes about
In the slimiest clefts.

His bubbling plume
Surrenders to currents,

No one watches
Its sud on the surface.

3   He's slipped away
     Beyond blueprints and planned dives.

     When he rises
     There's no audience or foreman

     Owns or tells him.
     He's nobody's feeler

     For drownings or
     Sinkings or loose bridges.

     It's come to be
     He just loves the water.

4   The straitjacket
     Of clock and calendar

     Dissolves, the bed
     Of the river is soft—

     It's not overtime
     Keeps him here at all.

     The air's a slap
     In the face. He always

     Walks home late now
     In rubber and goggles.

                                   SEAMUS HEANEY

❧ Girl with 'Cello

There had been no such music here until
A girl came in from falling dark and snow
To bring into this house her glowing 'cello
As if some silent, magic animal.

She sat, head bent, her long hair all a-spill
Over the breathing wood, and drew the bow.
There had been no such music here until
A girl came in from falling dark and snow.

And she drew out that sound so like a wail,
A rich dark suffering joy, as if to show
All that a wrist holds and that fingers know
When they caress a magic animal.
There had been no such music here until
A girl came in from falling dark and snow.

MAY SARTON

Boxer

Poised, relaxed, as a cat that waits,
   Too obviously bored, for the mouse to venture,
You endure the familiar ritual. They lace
   The gloves on, lead you to the center,
The half-heard mutter and the touching hands.
   The lights insist upon your thinning hair,

The best years are behind. Nothing at stake
   Tonight; purse and crowd are small;
Only another fight among the hundred odd
   Since boyhood and the animal
Tumblings in the street. Never a champion:
   You fought him once, but lost the call;

And not again. These are the final years
   As the ageing body threatens to rebel
And they send the upstart boys to take you.
   One will. But not tonight. The bell
Calls you to work, and to your finest night.
   The crowd held silent by your fluent spell,

For once not screaming for the knockout punch
   You never had, watches an adept in an art
That, like an actor's, lives in the splendid moment
   And the betraying memory. You dart
The left hand like a bird that, roused to danger,
   Rakes at the hunter's eyes, and start

The young blood flowing as the right hand pounds
   The ribs and belly and you move away,
Then in, tense and pure and timeless
   In your perfect dance. Coolly you display
The repertoire of moves and punches mastered
   Through the dull years of sweat for pay.

You win. Time, masked as this beaten boy,
   Has his hand shaken and his matted hair
Ruffled by your glove. You shower, dress,
   Quietly collect your winner's share,
And leave, a tired workman going home,
   Who carved a marble image on the air.

JOSEPH P. CLANCY

❧ Art Student

With ginger hair dragged over
          fiery orange face
Blue shirt, red scarf knotted around his neck,
Blue jeans, soft leather Russian boots
Tied round with bands he ties and unties when
His feet are not spread sprawling on two tables—
Yawning, he reads his effort. It's about
A crazy Icarus always falling into
A labyrinth.

          He says
He only has one subject—death—he don't know why—
And saying so leans back scratching his head
Like a Dickensian coachman.

          Apologizes
For his bad verse—he's no poet—an art student—
—Paints—sculpts—has to complete a work at once
Or loses faith in it.

          Anyway, he thinks
Art's finished.
          There's only one thing left
Go to the slaughter house and fetch
A bleeding something-or-other—oxtail, heart,
Bollocks, or best a bullock's pair of lungs,
Then put them in the college exhibition,
On a table or hung up on a wall

Of if they won't allow that, just outside
In the courtyard.

    (Someone suggests
He put them in a plastic bag. He sneers at that.)

The point is they'll produce some slight sensation—
Shock, indignation, admiration. He bets
Some student will stand looking at them
For hours on end and find them beautiful
Just as he finds any light outside a gallery,
On a junk heap of automobiles, for instance,
More beautiful than sunsets framed inside.
That's all we can do now—send people back
To the real thing—the stinking corpse.

STEPHEN SPENDER

A Character

Summers, in hospital whites, he takes your breath away
strolling with the incredible deftness of an eland
among merchants, schoolboys at jab-and-scramble
    play,
waddling girls, the usual stink and bustle of the streets.
He stretches, easily, onto the balls of his feet
as if he might get soiled, or might recall an errand
and sail out like a white heron, someone from another
    planet,
dimension, some pure merciful visitor, reincarnate.

Asked for his rent, he hasn't the faintest
    comprehension,
but will pass on without so much as disapproval
of this corrupt town. His is that intense preoccupation
one sees in nuns or eighteenth century fops.
He frequents only the most fashionable of the shops
neither to buy nor sell; beyond good and evil,
he saunters along the aisles, lifting the cunningest
little things—his own by right of natural good taste.

And hasn't he, after all, the right—no, almost the
    duty—
to take care that such fine things are not neglected
in the hands of those who couldn't appreciate them
    truly?
And after all, if you think what he has suffered,
it is no more than just that he should recover

138

the few small things he has been able to collect?
Surely a man needs some haven, some small fortress
against manifest vulgarity and worldliness?

His throw rugs and furniture are all in whites;
lately, he's done the walls white like a physician's
consultation room. He sits up languishing, nights,
cleaning his nails, or lies down to inspect his injuries
since, though he lives immaculately, he's
developed a strange susceptibility to lesions
apparently of some old wound he's liable to forget.
He thinks the world is his scab and picks at it.

W. D. SNODGRASS

It's neither black nor white
and lives beneath a stone—
writhes out only at night—
touch it and it's gone
boring deeper down;
it knows what's wrong and right,
likes a backwoods ground
but also thrives in cities
and hides in every town;
velvet in its stealth,
it couples in the dark,
secretly feeds on filth,
avoiding human pities—
pretends to mean no harm
except as a defense,
but poisoner of life,
at either of its ends
it has a lethal mouth.

HAROLD WITT

❧ The Umpire

Everyone knows he's blind as a bat.
Besides, it's tricky to decide,
As ball meets mitt with a loud splat,
Whether it curved an inch outside
Or just an inch the other way
For a called strike. But anyway,
Nobody thinks that just because
Instead he calls that close one Ball,
That that was what it really *was*.
(The pitcher doesn't agree at all.)

His eyes are weak, his vision's blurred,
He can't tell a strike from a barn door—
And yet we have to take his word.
The pitch that was something else before
(And *there's* the mystery no one knows)
Has gotten to be a ball by now,
Or got to be called ball, anyhow.
All this explains why, I suppose,
People like to watch baseball games,
Where Things are not confused with Names.

WALKER GIBSON

✌§ You Understand the Requirements

We are
sorry to have to
regret to
tell you
sorry sorry
regret sorry that you have
failed

your hair should have been
piled up higher

you have failed to
pass failed
your sorry
regret your
final hair comprehensive
exam satisfactorily
you understand the requirements

you understand we are
sorry final

and didn't look as professional
as desirable
or sorry dignified
and have little enough
sympathy for 16th century
sorry english anglicanism

we don't know doctoral
competency what to think and
regret you will sorry not
be able to stay
or finish

final regret your disappointment
the unsuccessfully completed best
wishes for the future
it has been a
regret sorry the requirements
the university policy
   please don't call us.

LYN LIFSHIN

VIII

---

why don't you write?

Wolves

I do not want to be reflective any more
Envying and despising unreflective things
Finding pathos in dogs and undeveloped handwriting
And young girls doing their hair and all the castles of
    sand
Flushed by the children's bedtime, level with the shore.

The tide comes in and goes out again, I do not want
To be always stressing either its flux or its permanence,
I do not want to be a tragic or philosophic chorus
But to keep my eye only on the nearer future
And after that let the sea flow over us.

Come then all of you, come closer, form a circle,
Join hands and make believe that joined
Hands will keep away the wolves of water
Who howl along our coast. And be it assumed
That no one hears them among the talk and laughter.

LOUIS MACNEICE

❧ Julia's Room

He went up the dark stairs and knocked at Julia's
    door;
It opened, and a blade of light cut the dim hall,
But the girl was a stranger, and when he spoke to her
She could not—or would not—understand at all.
She looked at him a moment—horrified, he thought—
Then slammed the door shut.

Bewildered, he guessed that while he was away
Julia must have invited a friend he had never known;
Sometimes when she asked an old friend to stay
She moved to the attic room and gave up her own.
So he climbed the second flight, but that floor was dark
As rain-drenched bark.

"Julia!" he called, but no light flashed on.
"Julia!" he called down the stair-well gloom.
. . . "Whoever you are, for God's sake be gone!"
The strange woman cried from Julia's own room.
Then he remembered it was fifty years ago,
And he melted like snow.

ROBERT HILLYER

❧ Passing Remark

In scenery I like flat country.
In life I don't like much to happen.

In personalities I like mild colorless people.
And in colors I prefer gray and brown.

My wife, a vivid girl from the mountains,
says, "Then why did you choose me?"

Mildly I lower my brown eyes—
there are so many things admirable people
do not understand.

WILLIAM STAFFORD

ఆ Girl in the Empty Nightgown

He had watched her slow-becoming:
    ample apron of a wife—
warm smell of cinnamon
    about her hair,
her sugar-cookie kisses
    for the children, looping loops.

When he was late for the eight-twenty-eight
    her crisp "good morning" curling
like the smell of bacon
    through the bedroom.
And at night, again, as basic as an egg,
    and looking up at him.
Their way upstairs his hand
    had lightly found her hip—
yeast-round and smooth—
    and when she rumpled into bed,
it was as if a basket
    of clean flannel nightgowns
had been toppled over,
    leaving one dazed, armless sleeve
caught on the edge. Before
    he turned the light out she sat up,
moved close to him and pulled her legs
    up under, with a pillowness
that made him wish the snow
    outside were wall-high and moat-wide.

But sometimes, only sometimes,
    he remembered that first day
in the forest, and she had moved like a flight
    of quick feathers—
surprise in her
    eyes.

ELOISE BRADLEY

You look
Like a classic geisha:
Your wooden pegs
Are her hair-ornaments,
Your white soundbox
Her moon-white face,
Your long, slim shank
Her thin
Elegant neck, elongated
As she intones
Some sad romance.
You both have catgut voices.

JAMES KIRKUP

ᥡ Dear Reader

Why don't you write you never
write each day I check the mail
nothing but truss ads and Christmas seals
Where are you what are you doing
tonight?
How are your teeth
when I brush mine blood
drips down my chin
Are you happy do you miss me
I will tell you
there is no-one like you
your eyes are unbelievable
your secrets are more interesting than anyone else's
you had an unhappy childhood
right?
I will rub your feet they're tired
I will say Hey
let's go to the movies
just the 2 of us

       love

PETER MEINKE

∛ The Photograph of the Unmade Bed

Cruelty is rarely conscious
One slip of the tongue

one exposure
among so many

a thrust in the dark
to see if there's pain there

I never asked you to explain
that act of violence

what dazed me was our ignorance
of our will to hurt each other

. . . .

In a flash I understand
how poems are unlike photographs

(the one saying *This coud be*
the other *This was*

The image
isn't responsible

for our uses of it
It is intentionless

A long strand of dark hair
in the washbasin

is innocent and yet
such thing have done harm

          : * * * * * *

These snapshots taken by ghetto children
given for Christmas

Objects blurring into perceptions
No 'art,' only the faults

of the film, the faults of the time
Did mere indifference blister

these panes, eat these walls,
shrivel and scrub these trees—

mere indifference? I tell you
cruelty is rarely conscious

the done and the undone blur
into one photograph of failure

          : * * * * * *

This crust of bread we try to share
this name traced on a window

this word I paste together
like a child fumbling

with paste and scissors
this writing in the sky with smoke

the silence

this lettering chalked on the ruins
this alphabet of the dumb

this feather held to lips
that still breathe and are warm

1969

ADRIENNE RICH

ᏉᏋ Together

Because we do
All things together
All things improve,
Even weather.

Our daily meat
And bread taste better,
Trees greener,
Rain is wetter.

PAUL ENGLE

You see them from train windows
in little towns, in those solitary lights
all across Nebraska, in the mysteries
of backyards outside cities—

a single face looking up,
blurred and still as a photograph.
They come to life quickly
in gas stations, overheard in diners,

loom up and dwindle, families
from dreams like memories too
far back to hold. Driving by
you go out to all those strange

rooms, all those drawn shades,
those huddled taverns on the highway,
cars nosed-in so close they seem
to touch. And they always snap shut,

fall into the past forever, vast lives
over in an instant. You feed
on this shortness, this mystery
of nearness and regret—such lives

so brief you seem immortal;
and you feed, too, on that old hope—
dim as a half-remembered
phone number—that somewhere

people are as you were always
told they were—people who swim
in certainty, who believe, who age
with precision, growing gray like

actors in a high school play.

VERN RUTSALA

IX

---

to be alive

No, the serpent did not
Seduce Eve to the apple.
All that's simply
Corruption of the facts.

Adam ate the apple.
Eve ate Adam.
The serpent ate Eve.
This is the dark intestine.

The serpent, meanwhile,
Sleeps his meal off in Paradise—
Smiling to hear
God's querulous calling.

TED HUGHES

❧ Morning Song

Love set you going like a fat gold watch.
The midwife slapped your footsoles, and your bald cry
Took its place among the elements.

Our voices echo, magnifying your arrival. New statue.
In a drafty museum, your nakedness
Shadows our safety. We stand round blankly as walls.

I'm no more your mother
Than the cloud that distills a mirror to reflect its own
    slow
Effacement at the wind's hand.

All night your moth-breath
Flickers among the flat pink roses. I wake to listen:
A far sea moves in my ear.

One cry, and I stumble from bed, cow-heavy and floral
In my Victorian nightgown.
Your mouth opens clean as a cat's. The window square

Whitens and swallows its dull stars. And now you try
Your handful of notes;
The clear vowels rise like balloons.

SYLVIA PLATH

The Sportsman

Partridge and quail, of course. Occasional woodcock,
Snipe, odd rabbits, squirrels, crows, coot—in fact,
All superficial life in range; lock, stock
And double barrel. Acquainted mallards quacked,
Considerable geese veered, and the gun's impact
Was pleasant to his shoulder. What a flock
Of startling memories rose to re-enact
Each death in feathers falling like a rock!
Decembers in red flannel, cold but game,
He pioneered through bullet-spattered wood.
The generous heart cried *kill*. If poor of aim,
He used the knife to comfort when he could.
Then suddenly, for no conspicuous reason.
He up and shot himself—well out of season.

DAVID MCCORD

∼§ Let Me Die a Youngman's Death

Let me die a youngman's death
not a clean & inbetween
the sheets holywater death
not a famous-last-words
peaceful out of breath death

when I'm 73
& in constant good tumour
may I be mown down at dawn
by a bright red sports car
on my way home
from an allnight party

Or when I'm 91
with silver hair
& sitting in a barber's chair
may rival gangsters
with hamfisted tommyguns burst in
& give me a short back & insides

Or when I'm 104
& banned from the Cavern
may my mistress
catching me in bed with her daughter
& fearing her son
Cut me up into little pieces
& throw away every piece but one

Let me die a youngman's death
Not a free from sin tiptoe in
candle wax & waning death
not a curtains drawn by angels borne
'what a nice way to go' death

ROGER McGOUGH

To a Fighter Killed in the Ring

In a gym in Spanish Harlem
boys with the eyes of starved leopards
flick jabs at your ghost
chained to a sandbag.

They smell in the air the brief truth of poverty
just as you once did:
                    "The weak don't get rich."

You made good.
Probably you were a bastard,
dreaming of running men down in a Cadillac
and tearing blouses off women.

And maybe in your dreams great black teeth
ran after you down dead-end alleyways
and the walls of your room
seemed about to collapse,
bringing with them a sky of garbage
and your father's leather strap.
and you sat up afraid you were dying
just as you had so many nights as a child.

Small bruises to the brain.
An accumulation
of years of being hit.

I will not forget that picture of you
hanging over the ropes, eyes closed,
completely wiped out.
Like a voice
lost in the racket of a subway train
roaring on under the tenements of Harlem.

LOU LIPSITZ

No poetic fantasy
but a biological reality,

a fact: I am an entity
like bird, insect, plant

or sea-plant cell;
I live; I am alive;

take care, do not know me,
deny me, do not recognise me,

shun me; for this reality
is infectious—ecstasy.

HILDA DOOLITTLE

Sand Dollar

This disc, stelliferous,
survived the tide
to tell us some small creature
lived and died;
its convex delicacy
defies the void
that crushed a vanished
echinoid.

Stoop down, delighted;
hoard in your hand
this sand-colored coin
redeemed from the sand
and know, my young sudden
archaeologist,
that other modes of being,
do exist.

Behold the horizon.
Vastness acts
the wastrel with
its artifacts.
The sea holds lives
as a dream holds clues;
what one realm spends
another can use.

JOHN UPDIKE

☙ Sniper

The tree becomes him, he becomes the tree—
A visionary whom the world can't see.

His solitude makes sense.
His leisure is immense.

Least organized of men and most unknown,
His deaths are singular, including his own.

How lean, how lyrical
A life. A fame how small.

ROBERT FRANCIS

❧ Soldier Asleep

Soldier asleep, and stirring in your sleep,
In tent, trench, dugout, foxhole, or swampy slough,
I pray the Lord your rifle and soul to keep,
And your body, too,

From the hid sniper in the leafy tangle,
From shrapnel, from the barbed and merciless wire,
From tank, from bomb, from the booby trap in the
    jungle,
From water, from fire.

It was an evil wind that blew you hither,
Soldier, to this strange bed—
A tempest brewed from the world's malignant weather.

Safe may you sleep, instead,
Once more in the room with the pennants tacked on
    the wall,
Or the room in the bachelor apartment, 17 L,
The club room, the furnished room across the hall,
The room in the cheap hotel,

The double-decker at home, the bench in the park,
The attic cot, the hammock under the willow,
Or the wide bed in the remembered dark
With the beloved's head beside you on the pillow.

Safe may the winds return you to the place
That howsoever it was, was better than this.

PHYLLIS McGINLEY

✑ The Asians Dying

When the forests have been destroyed their darkness
  remains
The ash the great walker follows the possessors
Forever
Nothing they will come to is real
Nor for long
Over the watercourses
Like ducks in the time of the ducks
The ghosts of the villages trail in the sky
Making a new twilight

Rain falls into the open eyes of the dead
Again again with its pointless sound
When the moon finds them they are the color of
  everything

The nights disappear like bruises but nothing is healed
The dead go away like bruises
The blood vanishes into the poisoned farmlands

Pain the horizon
Remains
Overhead the seasons rock
They are paper bells
Calling to nothing living

The possessors move everywhere under Death their star
Like columns of smoke they advance into the shadows
Like thin flames with no light
They with no past
And fire their only future

W. S. MERWIN

He doesn't know the world at all

Who stays in his nest and doesn't go out.
He doesn't know what birds know best
Nor what I want to sing about,
That the world is full of loveliness.

When dewdrops sparkle in the grass
And earth's aflood with morning light,
A blackbird sings upon a bush
To greet the dawning after night.
Then I know how fine it is to live.

Hey, try to open up your heart
To beauty; go to the woods someday
And weave a wreath of memory there.
Then if the tears obscure your way
You'll know how wonderful it is

To be alive.

AN ANONYMOUS CHILD
IN TEREZIN CONCENTRATION
CAMP, 1941

X

endpiece

Ithaca

When you start on your journey to Ithaca,
then pray that the road is long,
full of adventure, full of knowledge.
Do not fear the Lestrygonians
and the Cyclopes and the angry Poseidon.
You will never meet such as these on your path,
if your thoughts remain lofty, if a fine
emotion touches your body and your spirit.
You will never meet the Lestrygonians,
the Cyclopes and the fierce Poseidon,
if you do not carry them within your soul,
if your soul does not raise them up before you.

Then pray that the road is long.
That the summer mornings are many,
that you will enter ports seen for the first time
with such pleasure, with such joy!
Stop at Phoenician markets,
and purchase fine merchandise,
mother-of-pearl and corals, amber and ebony,
and pleasurable perfumes of all kinds,
buy as many pleasurable perfumes as you can;
visit hosts of Egyptian cities,
to learn and learn from those who have knowledge.

Always keep Ithaca fixed in your mind.
To arrive there is your ultimate goal.
But do not hurry the voyage at all.
It is better to let it last for long years;

and even to anchor at the isle when you are old,
rich with all that you have gained on the way,
not expecting that Ithaca will offer you riches.

Ithaca has given you the beautiful voyage.
Without her you would never have taken the road.
But she has nothing more to give you.

And if you find her poor, Ithaca has not defrauded
you.
With the great wisdom you have gained, with so much
experience,
you must surely have understood by then what Ithacas
mean.

C. P. CAVAFY

indices

☙ Authors and Titles

❧ First Lines